Original title:
Willow's Witty Whispers

Copyright © 2025 Creative Arts Management OÜ
All rights reserved.

Author: Miriam Kensington
ISBN HARDBACK: 978-1-80567-302-6
ISBN PAPERBACK: 978-1-80567-601-0

Enchanted Echoes of Lushness

In a grove where giggles play,
Leaves chuckle as they sway,
Mossy beds where whispers dwell,
Nature's secrets weave a spell.

Breezes tease with mischief's grin,
Dancing shadows pull you in,
Tiny critters share a jest,
Forest fun is at its best.

Sunbeams wink through leafy hues,
Twirling sprites sing silly blues,
Giggles bounce from branch to root,
Joyful laughter in pursuit.

Every rustle, every sound,
Nature's humor all around,
In this realm of vibrant cheer,
Laughter's language, loud and clear.

Jests in the Jade Wilderness

Amidst the trees, a prankster waits,
Crafty tales the forest fates,
Twigs and branches play their roles,
Binding laughter to our souls.

Bubbles burst from dewy ferns,
Mischief hides, and kindness earns,
Hopping hares with sneaky grins,
Chasing tales where joy begins.

Squirrels giggle, tap their feet,
Telling stories bittersweet,
Rivers chuckle, round they flow,
With every ripple, laughter grows.

Underneath the jade expanse,
Nature invites us all to dance,
Each step holds a playful tease,
In the wilderness, let's be free.

Silhouettes of Simple Joys

In twilight's glow, the whispers glide,
Casting shadows where dreams reside,
Simple joys twirl with delight,
As stars begin their playful light.

Crickets croon their evening tunes,
Underneath the watchful moons,
Fireflies flash a cheeky wink,
Nature's fun sparks thoughts to think.

Gentle winds tease the daisies,
Twisting blooms into crazies,
Laughter echoes in the night,
Bringing joy from purest light.

With every sigh, a jest in tune,
Underneath the silver moon,
Come gather 'round, let spirits soar,
In silhouettes, love's laughter pours.

The Enchantment of Nature's Lullaby

In crooning woods, the soft winds hum,
Bees buzz with laughter, oh so dumb,
Rustling leaves share secret tales,
Nature's charm never fails.

A brook giggles, tickles the shore,
Round the bend, it begs for more,
Pebbles grin, they jest and play,
In these games, we find our way.

Clouds above play hide and seek,
Whispers of joy they always leak,
With every breeze, a chuckle clear,
Filling hearts with endless cheer.

So close your eyes, let dreams alight,
Nature's lullaby, pure delight,
In every note, a playful sound,
In this world of joy, we're bound.

Conversations with the Wind

A breeze tickles the leaves above,
Sending secrets of mischief and love.
Whispers of giggles, a soft clap,
The trees join the fun in a playful rap.

Clouds drift by, wearing a frown,
The wind spins jokes that turn them around.
Laughter floats high, so light and free,
Nature's own stand-up, just wait and see.

Flowers dance, they sway to the beat,
On this stage, nature's comic retreat.
With every gust, the stories unfold,
Tales of laughter, both funny and bold.

In the hush of the evening, it's clear,
Those giggling gusts are all we hear.
The sky rolls its eyes at the playful scene,
As the wind plots more with mischievous glee.

Soft Serenades of Nature

The brook babbles tales, oh so sly,
While frogs in tuxedos croak and comply.
Crickets chirp, adding their tune,
In night's concert under the moon.

Leaves rustle as if sharing a joke,
A feathered friend joins in, quite a bloke.
Swaying grass joins the fun on cue,
All in nature, a comedy crew.

Stars twinkle above, tiptoeing bright,
Sparkling laughter fills up the night.
The owls take turns cracking a quip,
In this symphony, all nature's hip.

With giggles of petals, the roses chime,
In this melodious dance, no need for rhyme.
The hues of dusk paint mischievous schemes,
Where humor and nature weave silly dreams.

The Art of Silent Conversations

In the shade of branches, a whisper flows,
Thoughts exchanged with the tiniest prose.
Beneath the boughs, giggles softly tingle,
Nature's camera, capturing each jingle.

Squirrels plot pranks without a sound,
While butterflies flit, their laughter unbound.
The stillness hums with mischievous zest,
Every creature knows how to jest.

A silent chuckle from stones worn with time,
Rocks share tales that are truly sublime.
Behind every pause, a punchline awaits,
Jests wrapped in silence, unspoken fates.

In every rustle, a tale gently spins,
The secrets of nature held close in its sins.
With twinkling eyes, each moment so bright,
These whispers of laughter bring pure delight.

Playful Breezes and Swaying Dreams

The wind tickles cheeks, a cheeky tease,
With each airy touch, it dances with ease.
Breezes swirl round, in spirited flight,
Spreading giggles amid day and night.

Dandelions dream of their fluffy parade,
While the tall grasses join the masquerade.
Each puff tells a joke, oh what a scene,
As the sun plays tag, from gold to green.

Clouds puff out, with a woosh and a grin,
Their shapes morph into creatures, laughter akin.
In the sky's canvas, absurdity reigns,
With colors of humor flowing through veins.

In this playful waltz, where nothing feels coy,
Even the raindrops decide to enjoy.
Memories swirl in a whimsical gale,
Nature's lighthearted, vibrant tale.

Whimsy in the Woodland Air

In the forest where the trees sway,
The squirrels chat in a merry way.
Critters giggle with a sport-filled air,
As the sun dances upon their hair.

A fox in shoes struts with style,
A rabbit hops, it's quite a while.
The hedgehog juggles acorns round,
And all around, laughter does abound.

The owls hoot in rhythmic time,
Making jokes that are oh-so-prime.
With every ripple, a quirky cheer,
Nature's jesters bring good vibes near.

In every nook, a jest is found,
Where silly sounds make a joyful sound.
The woodland whispers, a playful tease,
Life here is meant to tickle with ease.

Echoing Tales of the Grove

Under branches rich with lore,
Berry wearing birds sing for more.
Each giggle echoes, where all gather,
In the grove where joy does shatter.

The beetles wear their hats askew,
While chipmunks plan their next sneak view.
A game of tag unfolds so bright,
As shadows dance beneath the light.

Mice debate, 'What cheese is best?'
While ants serve snacks, and never rest.
The wind carries a chuckling breeze,
As laughter bounces from tree to leaves.

Joyful tales flow like wild streams,
Tickled spirits live in dreams.
In this grove, where mirth expands,
Life's a jester with open hands.

Laughter in the Lattice of Leaves

Among the leaves, a secret sings,
Of frolic, fun, and tiny things.
Each rustling leaf tells a joke,
As little critters share the smoke.

A hedgehog dances with a flair,
While fireflies form a giggling pair.
Bunnies bounce with frenetic glee,
Chasing shadows, wild and free.

In the twilight, shadows enlarge,
Where playful whispers start to charge.
A raccoon pranks with stealthy grace,
In a world that's a comic chase.

Each moment's filled with sweet delight,
Under stars that giggle at night.
Laughter drips like sweetest honey,
In the lattice, all things are funny.

Tranquil Tales of Time

Beneath the branches, time takes flight,
With stories woven, soft as night.
The brook chuckles with every bend,
While stones keep secrets, without end.

A turtle grins, slow yet sly,
While ants march on, oh me, oh my!
The world spins like a merry wheel,
In tranquil moments, laughter feels real.

A sloth hangs low with a lazy wink,
Delighting in nonsense more than we think.
The wind carries tales of glee,
In this haven, forever carefree.

With each tick, the joy does rise,
As clouds giggle in the skies.
In quaint corners, time stands still,
With tranquil laughs, life's gentle thrill.

Unspoken Words of the Forest

In the grove where secrets play,
Trees giggle as they sway.
Squirrels dance with nimble cheer,
Joking with the birds so near.

Beneath the sun's bright, golden beam,
The brook gurgles a funny dream.
Leaves rustle with a cheeky sigh,
Echoes of laughter flutter by.

A chatterbox, the forest speaks,
In riddles and in silly peaks.
Nature's jesters, bold and spry,
Tickle us as they flutter by.

Whimsical Shadows at Dusk

As day turns into playful night,
Shadows leap with pure delight.
Crickets chirp their giggling tunes,
Under the gaze of silly moons.

A raccoon snickers in the dark,
Winking bright, a twinkling spark.
Fireflies twirl in jubilant dance,
Inviting all to join their chance.

Every rustle holds a tease,
Nature's wit upon the breeze.
Under the stars, beneath the sigh,
The forest's laughter fills the sky.

The Language of Laughter

Bubbles of giggles fill the air,
Flowers wink in vibrant flare.
Mushrooms chuckle, round and stout,
While the breeze spins tales about.

A playful hawk loops in grace,
While frogs join in the ribbit race.
Every blade of grass a grin,
Nature's jesters, they begin.

In this realm of muzzled fun,
Laughter sparkles, bright as sun.
Every creature, big or small,
Hums along—it's a joyous call.

Breezy Melodies of the Earth

The wind hums soft, a cheeky tune,
Poking fun at the lazy moon.
Clouds giggle in the azure sky,
As daisies bow and butterflies fly.

With every breeze, a joke is told,
Leaves rustle, their laughter bold.
The mountains chuckle, wide and stout,
Welcoming all with a joyful shout.

Laughter ripples through the stream,
Where dreams flow on like a lively theme.
As nature sings her silly song,
We dance, we laugh—where we belong.

Sprightly Secrets of the Sylvan

In the woods where laughter rings,
A squirrel jests with acorn flings.
The owls chuckle in the night,
As fireflies dance, a twinkling sight.

Beneath the trees in shades of green,
A fox tells tales, some quite obscene.
The grasses sway, they seem to grin,
As mischief brews with cheeky spin.

Nimble nymphs upon the brook,
Share stories from a hidden nook.
A rabbit hops with leaps so grand,
Crafting chaos—what a band!

A breeze brings giggles, light and free,
As petals swirl, a jubilee.
Each shade a canvas, colors bright,
In sprightly secrets, pure delight.

Frolics Among the Ferns

In a patch where ferns take flight,
A raccoon dances through moonlight.
With tiny spins and twirls so sweet,
He skips around on little feet.

The crickets chirp a silly tune,
As frogs join in, a jovial croon.
The ladybugs share jokes so sly,
While fluttering by, they wink an eye.

Among the leaves, a whisper flies,
A tangle of mischief 'neath the skies.
With teasing sprigs and sways so grand,
The ferns conspire, a crafty band.

Giggling mushrooms join the fun,
As shadows stretch when day is done.
Each frolic bursts with laughter fierce,
In this realm where joy is pierced.

Twilight's Playful Serenade

At dusk when shadows start to play,
The critters gather, end of day.
A hedgehog rolls in laughter's grasp,
While twilight's breeze gives light a clasp.

The stars peek out with cheeky grins,
As daytime's glee begins to spin.
A dance of vines, a lizard's leap,
Each wiggling form, a secret to keep.

The nightingale sings songs of glee,
While raccoons craft their late-night spree.
With every note, a chuckle plays,
As fireflies join in shimmering waves.

In this serenade of fun and jest,
Each creature knows they're truly blessed.
For laughter echoes in each sound,
In twilight's charm, joy is found.

The Gracious Dance of Tall Trees

In the breeze, they sway and sway,
Branches bent in a funny display.
Leaves giggle, tickle the air,
Nature's jesters, with flair to spare.

Roots tap-dance beneath the ground,
Mischievous whispers always abound.
With every creak, the laughter flows,
Echoing tales that no one knows.

Whispers Beneath the Canopy

Underneath a leafy dome,
Frogs croak secrets, feel like home.
Squirrels chime in, with nuts to share,
Jesters' court, in the cool night air.

A breeze laughs, as it calls my name,
Filling twilight with a playful game.
Rustling leaves, a giggling choir,
Joyful echoes of nature's fire.

Serene Murmurs in Twilight

In twilight's glow, the shadows grow,
Soft murmurs dance, as they steal the show.
Crickets chirp their nighttime tune,
As the stars wake up to swoon.

The moon winks down, a cheeky grin,
As whispers weave between the kin.
Mischief floats on the gentle wind,
Where every giggle is a new friend.

Laughter's Grace in the Green

The forest cracks with hearty glee,
Where laughter blooms in boughs so free.
Mossy carpets, soft and bright,
Hopscotch dreams under the moonlight.

Swaying limbs craft playful scenes,
A ballet of green in nature's jeans.
Mirthful breezes swirl and play,
In the grove, we'll laugh away.

Giggles Amongst the Green

In a patch of sunlit grass,
The frogs leap with delight,
They croak their jokes so loud,
No need for fear or fright.

Beneath a leaf so wide,
A squirrel tells a tale,
Of acorns lost and found,
And friends that never fail.

The ladybugs all laugh,
As their spots shine so bright,
A dance of tiny wings,
Bringing joy to the night.

With every rustling breeze,
The chuckles start to flow,
Nature's endless giggles,
In a playful, green show.

Whispers of Wisdom in the Woods

Beneath the ancient trees,
A rabbit gives a grin,
With stories filled with glee,
There's laughter deep within.

The owls hoot in delight,
As secrets start to spread,
Their wisdom wrapped in jokes,
To lighten any head.

The breeze teases the leaves,
Whisking fun through the air,
With every gentle rustle,
It tickles without care.

And in the heart of night,
The stars wink down with glee,
For in this woodland play,
All creatures dance so free.

Dances of Delicate Petals

In a garden full of blooms,
The petals swirl and sway,
They giggle in the sun,
Chasing clouds away.

The daisies wink and nod,
As butterflies join in,
With every graceful flutter,
They twirl and spin, then grin.

The bees buzz in delight,
As they share sweet, funny tales,
Of nectar, sun, and spring,
And how adventure sails.

With laughter in the air,
The blossoms dance and sway,
In this world of color,
Joy is here to stay.

The Joyful Secret Keeper

In the shadows of the trees,
A wise old fox does dwell,
With secrets oh so funny,
That only he can tell.

He chuckles with the breeze,
As whispers fill the air,
Of silly, cheeky pranks,
That lighten every care.

The crickets join the fun,
Creating tunes that cheat,
With their playful melodies,
They tap their little feet.

And in the hush of night,
The forest starts to grin,
For every secret shared,
Is laughter deep within.

Luminous Laughter in the Thicket.

In the shadows, giggles grow,
A tickle from the branches low.
Frisky squirrels glance with glee,
While chipmunks dance, wild and free.

The sunbeams play on leaves so bright,
Each rustle hides a silly sight.
A rabbit winks, spins in delight,
Turning the forest into pure light.

Pine cones tumble, a clumsy show,
While mossy cushions laugh below.
A toad sings out—a croaky tune,
Echoing under the laughing moon.

The breeze sways branches, a jolly band,
As nature's jokes take centered stand.
A chorus of chuckles fills the air,
In this thicket, joy's everywhere.

Secrets Beneath the Silken Leaves

Beneath the leaves, stories hide,
Whispers with the wind, they glide.
A crow cracks jokes, oh so sly,
While caterpillars laugh and try.

The flowers giggle when bees arrive,
Buzzing tales that come alive.
A breeze blows soft, a playful tease,
Where secrets dance among the trees.

A shadow darts, a tale unfolds,
The cheeky fox, so brave and bold.
He shares a pun with every leap,
Making the forest roar, not sleep.

In laughter's glow, the night's aglow,
The leaves nod gently, just so,
For nature's grins and chuckles sweet,
Are treasures found where silence meets.

Laughter Cradled in the Breeze

A playful breeze swirls all around,
With tickles that make the heart pound.
Leaves are jests, flutter and sway,
As nature's clowns begin to play.

A gentle rustle, a soft giggle,
A playful nudge, what a wiggle!
The daisies bow with chuckling grace,
While butterflies join the laughing race.

Squirrels perform in their acrobats,
Juggling acorns, what laughs in spats!
A wise old owl has tales to spin,
Of mischief and fun where all begin.

As shadows dance, the laughter grows,
With every breeze, the joy just flows.
A symphony of chuckles bright,
Beneath the stars, the world's alight.

The Whispering Grove of Thought

In a grove where giggles play,
Each rustle sparks a bright display.
Ideas dance on breezes swift,
Turning frowns to laughter's gift.

A gentle whisper from the trees,
Brings forth humor in soft pleas.
The wise old tree with wisecracks bold,
Shares stories of mischief, never old.

A garden party where jests are made,
With flowers blooming in joyous parade.
Each petal holds a smile so grand,
As bugs join in to make a band.

When dusk arrives, the echoes ring,
Of jolly jokes that nighttime brings.
In this grove, hilarity found,
With every whisper, joy knows no bound.

Silvery Sighs in the Moonlight

In the soft glow of the night,
Trees chuckle with delight.
Branches sway, they can't hide,
As shadows dance, side by side.

Crickets sing their silly song,
Nature's rhythm, never wrong.
The breeze carries laughter's call,
While stars twinkle, having a ball.

Owls hoot in humorous tones,
Tickling the air with funny groans.
A moonbeam trips and starts to slide,
Tickling the ground, where giggles reside.

As night deepens the playful jest,
Laughter drifts, it's a joyous fest.
Whispers float through the midnight air,
Every creature joins the fair.

The Charm of Nature's Banter

Leaves rustle in a playful song,
The trees laugh, it won't be long.
A squirrel shimmies, cheeks quite round,
While flowers nod, spinning 'round.

Clouds gather with a cheeky grin,
Winking down, let the fun begin.
Bee's buzz adds a comical flare,
As thay dance in the sunlit air.

The babbling brook shares a joke,
With pebbles giggling, trying to stoke.
A frog leaps high in delight,
Croaking chuckles throughout the night.

Nature's charm is a playful twist,
In every corner, you can't resist.
With laughter plastered across the skies,
The spirit of joy is never shy.

Beneath the Vine's Cheeky Gaze

Twisting vines with smirks so wide,
Wink at the moon, cannot hide.
Grapes giggle as they ripple down,
A teasing shade to nature's crown.

Bees zipped by with a merry buzz,
Sipping nectar, causing a fuss.
Each leaf rustles like a sweet delight,
As whispers unfold in the warm twilight.

The owl, a joker, hoots aloud,
Pulling pranks on the twilight crowd.
A funny jest in every breeze,
With nature at play, it aims to please.

Underneath the playful guise,
Existence sparkles with laughter's prize.
Beneath the vine's enchanting gaze,
The world erupts in silly praise.

The Veil of Mischievous Murmurs

In the shadow of twilight's embrace,
Whispers tease with a playful grace.
The crickets snicker, the frogs agree,
While fireflies dance, full of glee.

A rustle in the bushes hides,
A gathering of critters, oh, what pride!
Their stories tumble in a cheerful tone,
As laughter spills from their leafy throne.

The night wraps all in a humorous spell,
With every tickle, it wishes well.
Each voice plays a merry part,
In nature's choir, a cheeky heart.

The veil of murmurs drifts so free,
Inviting joy, come join the spree!
In every nook, there's fun to find,
As the night whispers, "Be of kind."

Dappled Dreams of the Happy Grove

In the shade where shadows play,
A squirrel winks and runs away.
The breeze giggles as it goes,
Tickling flowers, making them doze.

The sunbeams dance in playful arcs,
While rabbits hop and chase the sparks.
Laughter bubbles from the brook,
A joyous tune in every nook.

Birds are gossiping up high,
With silly tales that make us sigh.
A funky beetle starts to spin,
With groovy moves, let the fun begin!

In this grove where joy takes flight,
Every moment feels so bright.
Nature's jesters sing and sway,
As day turns to a funny play.

Gentle Hip-Hop of the Highlands

Up in the highlands, tunes arise,
A playful rhythm, oh what a surprise!
The fox prances with a grin so wide,
While sheep get groovy, caught up in the tide.

Grasshoppers jump in perfect time,
Tapping feet like a nursery rhyme.
The hills echo with jokes and jests,
As nature gathers, forgetting its debts.

A dark cloud floats, but brings no rain,
Just a silly hat for the farmer's pain.
Laughing daisies in a soft ballet,
Twisting and twirling in a bright display.

So join the dance, let spirits soar,
In highland humor, we all want more.
With every leap and every skip,
Life's an adventure, let's take a trip!

Whimsical Harmonies in the Hues

In a palette of green, pink, and blue,
Nature whispers secrets, known to a few.
A purple cat with polka-dot shoes,
Struts down the lane, spreading the blues.

Mirthful rainbows arch with glee,
As colors converse near the old pine tree.
Ladybugs laugh at a butterfly's plight,
Flapping about in the fading light.

A jolly frog croaks silly rhymes,
Echoing the joy of happier times.
Bright sunflowers nod their wise heads,
In a world where laughter steadfastly spreads.

With each brush stroke of the day,
Whimsical tones lead us astray.
In this artful realm where we play hide,
Laughter's the key and joy is our guide.

Lush Laughter Among the Leaves

Among the leaves where giggles crawl,
A bustling ant narrates it all.
With leafy cushions underfoot,
The trees join in with a mellow hoot.

Sunsets splash like a painter's brush,
Where whispers blend with evening's hush.
A chubby raccoon sings a tune,
Making the stars giggle and swoon.

Breezes carrying jokes on their wings,
As owls chuckle, sharing their flings.
While vines swing low with cheeky cheer,
Laughter reverberates—oh so near!

In this luscious grove of delight,
Every moment sparkles so bright.
Wonders await in every nook,
Join in the fun, take a look!

Nature's Playful Elegance

Beneath the draping greens, they play,
A dance of shadows through the day.
The branches sway, a laughing tune,
Where sunlight filters, bright as noon.

In the breeze, a giggle's heard,
As petals flutter, quite absurd.
The squirrels chase, all in a rush,
While butterflies join in the hush.

Oh, how the flowers seem to tease,
Dressed in colors, bright as peas.
They wink at bugs, with charm so rare,
And sway about with style and flair.

In nature's court, the jesters thrive,
Where every leaf can come alive.
With every rustle, life's a jest,
In this bright world, we're truly blessed.

Mischief Beneath the Boughs

Underneath the branches' seam,
The critters plot, they scheme and dream.
A acorn tumbles, rolling fast,
Laughing as it hits the grass.

The rabbit hops with cheeky glee,
Chasing shadows, wild and free.
A sneaky crow steals a bright hat,
And giggles softly, just like that.

The whispers of the breeze conspire,
To fan the flames of woodland fire.
A ticklish tick, a playful nudge,
With nature's charm, we can't begrudge.

And in the dark, the fireflies beam,
As laughter echoes, sweet as cream.
Beneath the boughs, in joyful dance,
The world's a stage, a merry chance.

The Flutter of Joy

Amidst the daisies, laughter blooms,
A symphony of teasing tunes.
The ladybugs hold tiny shows,
With wiggly moves, they steal the prose.

The wind, a prankster, tells the trees,
To shake their leaves and toss the peas.
While bees buzz by with silly flair,
Dancing through the fragrant air.

A timid hare peeks from his shroud,
To join the fun, so brave, so loud.
With tiny hops, he swirls around,
Creating joy where peace is found.

Each flutter whirls, a merry sight,
With whispers dancing in the light.
In every bloom, a chuckle plays,
In nature's humor, we find our ways.

Enchanted Echoes of the Glade

In glades where sunlight gently beams,
The whispers weave their playful dreams.
Old logs chuckle, mossy and wise,
As dragonflies perform their highs.

The mushrooms sport their polka dots,
As shadows dally in sunny spots.
Each ripple sings a silly song,
Inviting all to dance along.

With every rustle, joy's declared,
An ancient joke, a secret shared.
Where nature giggles, moods take flight,
Transforming day with pure delight.

So gather round, let laughter swell,
In glades where friendships find their spell.
With every echo, purest play,
In enchanted woods, we drift away.

Whims of the Whispering Woods

In the woods where whispers play,
The trees chuckle in a funny way.
Squirrels dance on branches high,
Telling tales as the birds fly by.

A rabbit wears a flashy hat,
While owls hoot and cats do chat.
Leaves twirl like dancers in the breeze,
Making mischief with utmost ease.

The mushrooms giggle, pink and stout,
While butterflies flutter about.
Every rustle is a joke well spun,
In this forest, laughter's never done.

So if you hear a giggle near,
Join the fun, shed a tear of cheer.
Nature's jesters under the sun,
Inviting all to laugh and run.

Whirling Dreams in the Canopy

In the canopy, dreams take flight,
With critters jesting day and night.
A fox in glasses reads the news,
While raccoons wear seven hues.

The branches sway like giddy friends,
As the day to night transcends.
A trickster breeze begins to tease,
And makes the leaves laugh with ease.

Treetops chuckle, low and loud,
As the flowers sway, feeling proud.
But watch out for the cheeky crow,
Who steals your snack, just for show!

Dreams whirling round in leafy flight,
With giggles echoing in the night.
Nature's cloaked in joyous schemes,
Enthralling all in whimsical dreams.

Chimes of Cheer in the Chill

When the chill sets in, bells do ring,
With jolly tunes the critters bring.
Snowflakes dance like playful sprites,
As laughter echoes through the nights.

Chirping crickets in winter's freeze,
Are making jokes with utmost ease.
A bear in boots slips and slides,
While the chilly air with smiles abides.

The evergreens wear frosty hats,
And the river sings with joyous chats.
Icicles glint like laughter's tears,
As frosty fun dispels all fears.

Chimes of cheer ring high and low,
In the crisp air, joy starts to flow.
Each frosty giggle, a merry thrill,
In the heart of winter, laughter will.

Laughter from the Leafy Veil

Behind the leaf curtain, whispers flow,
Crafting jokes in the sun's warm glow.
A spider spins tales with sticky thread,
As the daisies laugh, their petals spread.

In the leafy veil of vibrant green,
The forest holds a funny scene.
A chipmunk juggles acorns galore,
While frogs croak out a raucous roar.

Breezes tickle the boughs above,
As nature dances, spreading love.
Joyful echoes serenade the air,
In the leafy veil, humor's everywhere.

So venture forth, join the spree,
In the boughs and breezes, wild and free.
A world alive with giggles and glee,
Under the canopy, come and see!

The Voice of the Verdant

In the woods, the trees will chat,
Saying nonsense, imagine that!
A squirrel's tale, a crow's wise crack,
Whispers rustle, never slack.

The moss giggles underfoot,
Sharing secrets none can root.
A breeze that tickles, leaves that dance,
Nature's humor, a joyful chance.

Old oaks chuckle, branches sway,
Each leaf a jest, come out to play!
One tree claims it's a great sage,
While another shouts, "Join my stage!"

So listen close, in the glade,
Laughter lives where dreams are made.
In verdant realms, with mirth we roam,
In nature's heart, we'll find our home.

Breezy Whimsies and Wonder

Tickle the clouds, let laughter soar,
Playful secrets on a forest floor.
A chipmunk jests with a cheeky glance,
Every breeze is a joyful dance.

Dandelions blow with a puff of mirth,
Each tiny wish knows its worth.
Petals peek from shy, tucked beds,
Whispers of fun from nature's heads.

The brook babbles with a giggle or two,
While frogs croak songs, old and new.
Frisky ferns wave, "Come take a look!"
In this wild stage, they've got the hook.

So wander lightly, with joy on your path,
Catch every chuckle, share every laugh.
These whispers of wonder, breezy and bright,
Turn every walk into pure delight.

Radiant Revelries in the Greenery

In the orchard, ripe jesters grow,
Fruit-filled laughter, on branches aglow.
Grapes merrily roll in playful cheer,
Each harvest time brings jokes we hold dear.

Sunlight spills like a barrel of wine,
Laughter ripples in every vine.
Bumblebees buzz with a ticklish hum,
Calling all creatures; come join the fun!

As daisies wink in the soft sunrise,
And butterflies flaunt their colorful ties,
Let's dance through greens, so free and bold,
In revelries bright, our stories unfold.

With every giggle that leaves our lips,
Nature's comedy takes joyous trips.
So come explore where the wild things be,
And laugh along in this jubilee.

Forest Frolics and Fables

In the heart of the wood where stories spin,
A fox wears glasses, keen to begin.
"Did you hear? The owl lost a bet!
Now he's stuck with a feathered pet!"

The raccoons gather, tales to regale,
With nutty punchlines and a playful wail.
"Why did the pine tree wear a frown?
It couldn't find its way to town!"

So frolic we must through thickets and trails,
Chasing each other with giggles and flails.
The forest's alive, with joy all around,
In this tapestry woven from laughter unbound.

As dusk spills its glow on the woodland floor,
We cherish the tales, ever wanting more.
In fables of frolics, we take our rest,
With whispers of fun, it's truly the best!

Tales Spun from Gossamer Dreams

In the meadow where shadows dance,
The grass confesses to a trance.
A butterfly trips on its own wing,
As daisies giggle, oh what a fling!

The clouds wear hats made of fluff,
While ants march to jazz, oh so tough.
Squirrels plot with mischievous grins,
As acorns tumble like silly wins.

Under the moon, the crickets croon,
A raccoon spins tales by the light of noon.
With each twirl, the world spins round,
In laughter and cheer, joy can be found.

So let's weave tales that tickle the mind,
With quirky characters, one of a kind.
In whispers of joy, the night shall gleam,
As dreams and giggles blend in a stream.

The Leafy Laughter of Time

Leaves flutter down, a comical sight,
They tumble and roll, taking flight.
With every breeze, they chuckle and play,
In the dance of the branches, the world sways.

An old oak grins with wisdom untold,
Its bark a story, rich and bold.
Each knot and twist, a secret it keeps,
As squirrels dream up their laughter-filled leaps.

Time ticks by like a playful racquet,
While nature's clock gives a little clacket.
In giggles and sighs, the seasons will change,
A tapestry woven, both funny and strange.

So let's toast to the time that we share,
With laughter and fun filling the air.
In the leafy embrace, let's weave and unwind,
For joy in the journey is what we will find.

Serenades of the Gentle Woods

Amidst the trees, a waft of glee,
Where chipmunks dance as wild as can be.
With sticks for guitars, they sing their song,
In the serenade of the woods, we belong.

The brook babbles tales that tickle the ear,
As frogs jump in rhythm, spreading good cheer.
Hare flips a coin, but it lands on its nose,
While the trees let out giggles in breezy prose.

A picnic spread out for the critters, a feast,
With berries and nuts, they munch and they tease.
The badger cracks jokes, oh so astute,
While all around join in with a hoot!

Together they savor the moments of fun,
In nature's theater, awash with the sun.
With each passing whisper, a chuckle is shared,
In the gentle woods, laughter is laid bare.

Songs of the Swaying Sprigs

Sprigs sway softly, a comical crew,
Their movements a dance, both silly and true.
With the wind as conductor, they twirl and spin,
In nature's grand symphony, laughter begins.

Dandelions puff, sending wishes in flight,
While the grasshopper leaps amidst the daylight.
A flower poses, with petals so bright,
In the delightful chaos, all feels just right.

Bees buzz around with tales to impart,
Of nectar and blooms, a sweet work of art.
But a clumsy bug tips over a stem,
And giggles ensue in nature's dim gem.

So here's to the sprigs that brighten the day,
With whispers of joy in their own quirky way.
In this lively garden, let laughter arise,
As we dance to the tune beneath open skies.

Tender Secrets of the Sylvan

In the woods, the leaves conspire,
Squirrels giggle, spirits higher.
A fox tells tales of mishaps near,
While rabbits hop with no trace of fear.

Mushrooms dance in the morning glow,
Whispers tickle, where breezes blow.
A deer winks, oh what a sight,
While fireflies plan their late-night flight.

Trees remember each cheeky tale,
Breezes laugh, like a wind-swept sail.
Each shade has secrets, funny and bright,
A world alive with pure delight.

Gather close, beneath the bows,
Nature's stage, oh how it bows.
In this haven, joy does dwell,
Laughter echoes, a ringing bell.

Conversations with the Clouds

Fluffy forms up in the blue,
Chatting lightly, as they do.
One claims it's raining jellybeans,
The other dreams of flying machines.

A puffy cumulus takes a stand,
Says, "I'm the softest in the land!"
Thunder giggles, rumbling loud,
While lightning grins, all proud and bowed.

Wind joins in, with teasing grace,
Whirling 'round in a lively race.
"Catch me if you can!" it shouts,
As raindrops tumble and sway about.

In this skyward carnival fair,
Joyful whispers fill the air.
Clouds are jesters, bright and bold,
With funny stories never told.

Flickers of Joy in the Foliage

In the forest, laughter weaves,
Through tangled vines and rustling leaves.
A chipmunk gestures, "Just you wait,
I've hidden snacks for a wild debate!"

Sunlight dapples, a game of tag,
Where shadows dance, all in a brag.
"Did you hear the one about the tree?"
"Don't bark, it's a pun!" they shout with glee.

Breezes twirl in a merry spin,
Tickling spots where giggles begin.
Caterpillars wear tiny hats,
Inviting all, come join our chats!

Frogs croak jokes from the pond's edge,
Whilst crickets chirp a lively pledge.
In this green haven, mirth does bloom,
Nature's jesters always resume.

Lighthearted Murmurs of the Breeze

Cool whispers in the summer heat,
A gentle laugh, a playful tweet.
"Did you know the trees can dance?"
They sway with glee, in a lively trance.

Hummingbirds tease in a swift flight,
"Catch me if you can!"—what a sight!
Petals giggle as they flutter down,
Painting smiles all over town.

Laughter bubbles from the brook,
Singing songs in a happy nook.
"Why so glum?" a stone will say,
"Join our fun, come out and play!"

As the day fades, stars peep through,
The breeze whispers, "Here's something new!"
With every gust, a chuckle shared,
In a world where joy is declared.

Fluttering Fancies in the Ferns

In the ferns, a squirrel pranced,
Chasing shadows, he danced.
With a flick of his fluffy tail,
He tripped and turned to sail.

A ladybug in red attire,
Declared a contest, oh, so dire.
Who can soar and touch the sky?
But fell right down with a sigh.

Toads hopped with a croaky sound,
Creating giggles all around.
One slipped on a shiny stone,
And landed with a funny groan!

A chattering bird from the tree,
Sang a tune of pure glee.
All the critters joined the show,
In this ferny, fun-filled glow.

Joyful Antics Amongst the Treetops

High up where the breezes play,
Monkeys swing without delay.
One forgot how to let go,
And tumbled with a joyful "whoa!"

The owls watched with puzzled views,
While parrots shared silly news.
A squirrel brought a tiny snack,
And sent the monkeys into a wrack!

Bouncing branches showed their might,
As friends twirled in a woody flight.
A twig snapped, oh what a scene,
Down came a shower of beans!

Laughter echoed through the leaves,
As chums concocted sneaky thieves.
They hid behind the big oak crest,
Firmly planning their next jest!

Sublime Secrets in the Shimmering Shade

Under leaves where secrets gleam,
A grasshopper shared a dream.
He spoke of dancing in the rain,
But ended up caught in a chain!

A wise old turtle chimed in slow,
"Never dance where puddles grow!"
But the young insects hopped away,
Ignoring caution, come what may.

Bees buzzed near in playful strife,
Playing tag with the edge of life.
With every twist and every whirl,
They spun around in silly twirl!

Secrets spilled under the sun,
As laughter mingled, oh so fun.
In this shade of bravado's call,
They twinkled bright and gave their all.

The Melody of Mirth in the Meadow

In the meadow where daisies sway,
Frogs croaked a humorous ballet.
With leaps and bounds, they took their stance,
Each move became a funny dance!

A rabbit with a floppy ear,
Brought out carrots with great cheer.
"Who wants a treat?" he did proclaim,
But tripped and rolled without a shame!

The butterflies came, all in a row,
Twinkling bright in the sun's warm glow.
They tickled cows, who mooed in fits,
While sheep joined in with silly skits.

As day turned to dusk, laughter soared,
Every creature joyously roared.
In the meadow, where stories blend,
Mirthful moments never end!

Soft Shadows of Clever Echoes

In the glade where shadows play,
Jokes are whispered, light and gay.
Leaves chuckle with a gentle sway,
As laughter dances, brightens day.

A squirrel scampers, quick and spry,
Telling tales that make birds fly.
The breeze joins in, a breezy sigh,
Echoes of humor hanging high.

Glimmers of fun beneath the trees,
Nature teases, invites the breeze.
With each rustle, a playful tease,
Clever chats float with such ease.

Secrets tickle through the air,
As the playful critters share.
In this forest, joy is rare,
A canvas of laughter everywhere.

Beneath the Canopy of Cleverness

Underneath this leafy dome,
Mischief thrives, makes trees a home.
Chirps of laughter, bright and chrome,
A symphony of jest, a poem.

Branches stretch and sway with grace,
Whispers giggle, light their pace.
Nature's jesters find their place,
Creating smiles on every face.

The tiny ants march in line,
Sharing jokes, a clever design.
Each step forward, they align,
Marching to the beat, so fine.

Sunlight filters, playful beams,
Turning laughter into dreams.
In this haven, nothing seems,
As silly whispers turn to themes.

The Dance of Swaying Secrets

In the meadow, secrets swirl,
Around each petal, a playful twirl.
Nature's dance, a lively whirl,
With giggles curling, as joys unfurl.

Grasshoppers jump with cheeky flair,
Telling tales without a care.
Swaying leaves mockingly stare,
As sunlight catches in the air.

The flowers gossip, petals preen,
Wearing smiles so bright and keen.
A sweet duet of jokes unseen,
In this realm of fun, serene.

With each rustle, thoughts take flight,
In laughter's grip, all feels right.
By dusk's arrival, fading light,
The breezes join in, giddy night.

Leaves that Laugh in the Wind

Fluffy clouds drift, a gentle tease,
While leaves chuckle in the breeze.
With every twist, they whisper cheese,
Nature's humor, meant to please.

Little birds chirp clever lines,
As they flit through the playful pines.
A chorus of love in sweet designs,
Their laughter rings, soft as wines.

The sun winks through branches high,
As squirrels dance and jump nearby.
In this theater, no need to pry,
The jokes abound, and spirits fly.

Even shadows play their part,
With clever quips that touch the heart.
In every corner, laughter's art,
A canvas of fun, a joyful chart.

Twigs of Truth and Jest

In the forest, green and bright,
Trees hold secrets, hidden light.
Squirrels chatter, birds take flight,
Nature's laughter, pure delight.

Roots are grinning, branches sway,
Offering tricks in a playful way.
With each flutter, the critters play,
Whispers echo, come what may.

Frogs croak jokes, in the mud below,
Teasing each other with a show.
Leaves rustle softly, secrets flow,
In this garden, giggles grow.

Underneath the moon, shadows dance,
Every creature takes a chance.
With a whimsy, and a glance,
Stories bloom in a merry prance.

A Tangle of Playful Thoughts

Beneath the branches, thoughts entwine,
Laughter bubbles, sweet as wine.
A rabbit grins, with mischief fine,
In this realm, all things align.

Chipmunks play, with nuts to share,
While wise old owls pretend not to care.
Every chirp, a giggle's dare,
Nature thrives on gentle flair.

Dancing leaves in breezy jest,
Every creature's charming quest.
In the rustle, a joyful fest,
Echoes linger, never rest.

In the thicket, fun unspools,
Nature's laughter, breaking rules.
In the sunlight, life renews,
With fancy dreams and silly jewels.

Echoes of Enigmas in the Glade

In the glade, where shadows play,
Mysteries dance throughout the day.
Whispers flutter, come what may,
Curiosity leads the way.

A riddle here, a jesting dare,
Stone-faced hedgehogs catch the air.
Every flicker hides a flair,
In this woodland, secrets share.

Bubbles in the brook, make a sound,
Silly ducks waddle all 'round.
With every ripple, laughter found,
Nature's giggle knows no bound.

Among the ferns, and flowers bold,
Tales are woven, laughter told.
In the forest whispers, we behold,
Joy in secrets, bright and gold.

The Fables Taught by Nature

In the meadow, stories sing,
Fables taught by the birds in spring.
Each little note, a wise old thing,
Nature's laughter, a joyous fling.

Beneath the boughs, jokes take flight,
Critters scurry, morning light.
With every rustle, spirits bright,
Whimsy bounces, pure delight.

The ants march on, a comic line,
Carrying crumbs, perfectly fine.
In their hustle, fun's divine,
Life in nature, a grand design.

As shadows lengthen, tales unwind,
With bated breath, the young and blind.
In this circle, love we find,
Nature's fabric, hilariously kind.

Delightful Murmurs of the Meadow

In the grass, the crickets dance,
With a tune that's full of chance.
Breeze will tickle every blade,
As laughter in the sunlight played.

Bumblebees buzz like little jesters,
Wearing stripes like silly testers.
Flowers giggle in colors bright,
In a scene of pure delight.

A rabbit hops with pants too tight,
Chasing shadows, what a sight!
Frogs croak jokes with silly glee,
Echoing through the mighty tree.

Clouds above give sly remarks,
Scheming in their fluffy parks.
Nature hums a cheeky song,
Where all the world can sing along.

Secrets of the Swaying Brush

Gentle whispers in the breeze,
Tickle all the barks and leaves.
Squirrels chuckle, tail on high,
As they plot and prance nearby.

A sly raccoon with twinkling eyes,
Steals the snacks with quick surprise.
Behind the bush, he lets out yelps,
Laughing at the noise he helps.

The otters play in merry streams,
Chasing shadows, weaving dreams.
In the reeds, the frogs' loud cheer,
Reveals secrets we all hear.

Dancing daisies in their spots,
Wave hello and tie their knots.
In this brush, the fun won't cease,
Every glance a chance for peace.

Reverberations of Joy in the Wild

In the woods where giggles play,
Woodpeckers drum the day away.
Dancing leaves with tricks to share,
Chasing echoes on the air.

Ants parade with tiny hats,
Carrying crumbs like little brats.
A dandelion floats so bold,
Winks at tales just waiting to be told.

The sunbeams tease the coats of deer,
Making shadows disappear.
As laughter bubbles up from streams,
Nature giggles in its dreams.

Breezes dance and swirl with glee,
Tickling every little tree.
Every corner, joy abounds,
In the wild where fun resounds.

The Symphony of Serene Sighs

The river laughs with water's play,
Rhythmic splashes light the day.
Gentle waves hum sweetly warm,
Creating ripples, a soothing charm.

Owls give nods, their wisdom sly,
With a wink and a watchful eye.
In the canopy, leaves collide,
Whispered secrets that can't hide.

Flowers sway with grace so bold,
Serenade of hues unfold.
Bees and blooms in secret chat,
Stirring joy in every spat.

Under stars, the night takes flight,
Crickets chirp in pure delight.
Every sigh a joyous jest,
In nature's arms, we find our rest.

The Subtle Art of Nature's Jest

In the garden, a gnome winks,
Secretively plotting as he thinks.
The flowers giggle, sway with cheer,
While worms tell jokes, so loud and clear.

The trees hold hands, a grand parade,
While bees hum tunes that never fade.
Clouds toss a smile, round and soft,
As sunbeams dance and lift us aloft.

Chuckles in the Shade

Under the branches, a squirrel grins,
Telling tales of his little sins.
A picnic blanket, spread just right,
With ants marching forth, a funny sight.

The daisies nod, their heads in glee,
As butterflies gossip, wild and free.
In the shade, laughter spills, like a stream,
Nature's comedy, a whimsical dream.

Enchanted Whispers of the Wild

Frogs croak riddles, sharp and neat,
While crickets tap dance on their feet.
A fox slips by, with a cheeky grin,
Planning pranks where mischief begins.

The moon chuckles, a silver hug,
As owls tell secrets, snug as a bug.
Stars giggle softly, twinkling bright,
In this enchanted realm of delight.

The Riddle of Rustling Branches

Branches rustle, a playful tease,
A breeze plays games, tickling leaves.
Mice exchange smirks, plotting in haste,
While shadows dance, a comical chase.

Under the starlight, whispers abound,
The nature of laughter, joy unbound.
With every rustle, a story unfolds,
Of frolicking spirits, young and old.

Songs of Swaying Shadows

In the park where shadows play,
Laughter echoes, bright and gay.
A squirrel dances, tail so grand,
While kittens plot, a mischief band.

Raindrops drum on leaves like cheer,
Who would dance without a fear?
A duckling quacks a silly song,
As moonlit beams say, "Join along!"

A tangled vine decides to swing,
With whispers sweet, it starts to sing.
While flower petals laugh and sway,
They steal the show for just one day.

As shadows twist and spirits rise,
A playful fox with knowing eyes.
Jokes are tossed like breezy leaves,
In this realm where joy believes!

Gentle Breezes of Brilliance

Soft winds giggle through the trees,
Carrying tales on playful knees.
A bumblebee in fancy dress,
Buzzes jokes with pure finesse.

The grass tickles the toes of fate,
Ants parade, they celebrate.
A ladybug rolls down a hill,
She won't stop 'til she gets her fill.

Clouds make faces, oh what fun,
Sharing secrets under the sun.
With breezy sighs and winks so sly,
Nature's laughter flutters by.

Every rustle, every sway,
Unfolds humor in the day.
In this realm where nonsense grows,
Joyful whispers, everyone knows!

Secrets in the Rustling Leaves

Leaves conspire in playful moods,
Giggling softly, sharing goods.
A wise old owl, with winking eye,
Hears the jokes that drift and fly.

A beetle tells a witty tale,
As breezes pause, begin to sail.
Butterflies flutter with delight,
Dancing stories into the night.

Beams of sun play peek-a-boo,
Tickling flowers, painting blue.
The rhythm flows in nature's bounds,
As silly laughter knows no sounds.

From under roots where secrets thrive,
Joyful whispers come alive.
Join the dance, with nature blend,
In laughter's arms, the fun won't end!

Echoes of Enchanted Laughter

Beneath the arch of twisting vine,
Laughter echoes, oh so fine.
A mischievous wind starts to tease,
What funny tales will it release?

Jumping frogs in polka dots,
Croak their jokes in silly spots.
Fireflies wink, sharing a glow,
While busy ants just steal the show.

A moonbeam's grin, a playful stare,
Tickles the air with flair to spare.
With every rustle, giggles bloom,
In every shadow, joy finds room.

So let the nightcraft tales unfold,
In the darkness, mysteries sold.
With echoes bright and laughter near,
Life's charm whispers, loud and clear!

Breezy Delights and Gentle Murmurs

In the breeze, the leaves do laugh,
Swaying gently, a playful gaffe.
Funny stories dance on air,
Trees gossip, with much flair.

Squirrels plot their acorn heists,
With cheeky grins, they roll the dice.
Fluttering birds chip in with cheer,
Their chirps a joke between each ear.

Sunbeams tickle the flower beds,
As petals giggle, nodding heads.
Every rustle brings a smile,
Nature's wit stacks up the while.

Even the brook joins in the fun,
Bubbling laughter under the sun.
The world is bright with jests so sweet,
In this mirthful, sunny retreat.

The Mirth of Nature's Tongue

A chatty breeze stirs up delight,
It teases trees, both day and night.
Rabbits laugh at their own shadows,
Witty whispers from the meadows.

The clouds play tricks, in shapes they bend,
Creating stories that never end.
Bees buzz tales of flowers grand,
As nature giggles, hand in hand.

Butterflies sport their brightest hues,
Flitting by with whimsy views.
Each bloom blooms with a cheeky wink,
In this chatter, what do you think?

Even the rocks have much to share,
With silent chuckles, they sit and stare.
Taking in all the whimsy near,
Nature's laughter, we hold dear.

Curious Tales from the Green

In the garden, secrets unfold,
Every petal has a tale bold.
The sun winks, a glimmer bright,
And the daisies giggle with delight.

Ants form armies, with silly aims,
Marching proudly in their games.
With tiny hats, they strut and prance,
Claiming victory in their dance.

Frogs croak their jokes, in the pond,
Echoes of humor, of which we're fond.
Dragonflies dart, teasingly near,
With laughter bubbling, crystal clear.

Every leaf has a smirk to share,
As branches sway, a comical affair.
In nature's realm of green and sheen,
Life's a riot, bursting with sheen.

Whispers of Wisdom by the Water

By the water's edge, giggles collide,
The ripples dance with a cheeky slide.
Ducks quack jokes in a splish-splash way,
As laughter echoes throughout the day.

Pebbles chuckle beneath the wave,
As fish swim by, plotting to rave.
Unruly reeds join in the fun,
Gentle sways, 'till day is done.

The sun dips low, a golden blare,
Casting shadows with a humorous flair.
Each woodpecker knocks out a beat,
Nature's rhythm is a joyful treat.

In the twilight, whispers abound,
Stories of joy, and peace surround.
With every splash and flickering light,
Nature giggles, pure and bright.

The Whimsy of Sunlit Breezes

In the light, the laughter gleams,
Dancing leaves with playful themes.
Sunbeams tickle every stray,
Come and chase the clouds away.

Breezes hum a silly song,
While the flowers swish along.
Whispers tease the fluttering kite,
Chasing birds in pure delight.

In the meadow, giggles soar,
Butterflies knock on nature's door.
Jokes are swirling in the air,
Who can catch them? Does anyone dare?

On such days, the world seems bright,
Filled with joy and sheer delight.
Laughter echoes, joy awakes,
In the sunlight, nature quakes.

Cheerful Whispers of the Wilderness

In the woods, the critters cheer,
Silly stories seem to steer.
Squirrels chatter, rabbits hop,
Nature's giggles never stop.

Trees wear hats of leafy green,
Curly vines spin wild and keen.
Breezy banter fills the air,
Come, o woodland friends—if you dare!

Mushrooms giggle, shadows sway,
In their dance, they laugh and play.
Every rustle speaks of fun,
Join the chatter, you've just begun!

In every nook, joy finds its way,
Whispers of glee brighten the day.
Mother Nature's playful jest,
Leaves you smiling—what a quest!

The Delicate Tapestry of Nature

Threads of color, laughter spun,
Nature weaves her tales for fun.
In the garden, joy unfolds,
Every petal a joke retold.

Bumbles buzz with charming grace,
Tickling flowers in their place.
Sunset paints a grin so wide,
Nature's wit can't be denied.

Through the brush, a fox prances,
While the creek hums silly glances.
Each ripple holds a tale to tell,
Of woodland pranks and jokes so swell.

In this canvas, laughter thrives,
A vibrant world where fun survives.
Every sight, a playful tease,
In the dance of rustling leaves.

Moments of Joyful Solitude

When the world sits quiet here,
I hear whispers—oh, so near.
A gentle breeze makes me chuckle,
Nature's charm, my heart will snuggle.

In stillness, the shadows dance,
Branches sway—a merry trance.
Solitude with a wink and nod,
In the special space I trod.

Leaves rustle with secrets told,
In this haven, feeling bold.
Every sigh, a giggling stream,
Alone, yet wrapped in nature's dream.

Moments filled with bright surprise,
Where even quiet holds the skies.
Joy blooms softly all around,
In this stillness, love is found.

www.ingramcontent.com/pod-product-compliance
Lightning Source LLC
Chambersburg PA
CBHW051635160426
43209CB00004B/656